Silkie

Also by Anne-Marie Cusac:

The Mean Days, Tia Chucha Press, 2001.

Silkie

poetry by

Anne-Marie Cusac

*To Bailey,
Thanks for coming to the talk. Wishing you all good things.
Anne-Marie*

Many Mountains Moving Press
Longmont, Colorado
2007

© 2007 by Anne-Marie Cusac.
All rights reserved. Published 2007.
Manufactured in the United States of America.

Published by Many Mountains Moving Press.
www.mmminc.org.

Many Mountains Moving Press titles are distributed by Small Press Distribution, www.spdbooks.org.

Publishers Cataloging-in-Publication Data:
Cusac, Anne-Marie.
Silkie / Anne-Marie Cusac with an Introduction by Patrick Lawler.
— 1st ed.
ISBN-13: 978-1-886976-20-7.

Cover art by Adam Shaw, abshaw.com.
Design by Jeffrey Ethan Lee.
Copy editing by Bryan Roth.

Acknowledgements

Many Mountains Moving Vol. VII, 2006, for "wild enough," "silkie song," and "theft."

This book would not exist without the efforts of some who may not be its author, yet, through their careful attention, have made major contributions to the writing on these pages. Meg Schoerke read draft after draft, providing extensive editorial insights that ranged from broad and suggestive to small and specific. Without her clarity and willing criticism, I would not have been able to take an unwieldy batch of poems and create from it this story. Reginald Gibbons saw early on that *Silkie* was its own volume, rather than part of a larger project, traced the book's dramatic arc, and offered insights that helped to transform the last pages. The members of my poetry group in Madison, Wisconsin, critiqued drafts of the poems and the whole manuscript, offering me not only much needed help but also their great enthusiasm for the project. Finally, Jeffrey Ethan Lee of Many Mountains Moving Press and Patrick Lawler both provided extremely valuable editorial guidance, including some much needed prodding to write several new poems that added emotional depth to the story I was trying to tell.

For their spiritual support, I need to acknowledge my teachers past and present, my parents, and Cedar Marie. I am also grateful to my Canadian extended family for their stories, their cultural insights, and their affection through the decades.

My great thanks to all of you.

I would not have written this book without financial help from the city of Madison, Wisconsin, in the form of a CitiARTS Signature Grant, which enabled me to take a part-time leave from my work as a journalist. A Pleasant Rowland Fellowship for a month at Vermont Studio Center gave me the time and space to write the first draft. Finally, the steady support of Matthew Rothschild and the staff of *The Progressive* made it possible for me both to report for the magazine and to create *Silkie*.

For my dad, who took me to the ceilidh,
*and for the Maritimers who sing the old songs and tell the old stories,
with my gratitude and love.*

Introduction

by Patrick Lawler

If I had the time-energy, I would create a new discipline and call it Ecomythology in order to study, among other stories and myths, the exceptional book you have in your hands. This new discipline would explore the stories we tell ourselves through our mythical creations (centaurs, werewolves, and all manner of imaginary creatures) and how they shape our awareness of place and our relations to all animals and ourselves.

This is the power of this wonderful book by Anne-Marie Cusac. It captures a time when animals and human beings share desires and inhabit the same skins. This collection of poetry recounts the story of the Silkie (sometimes referred to elsewhere as Selkie), seals who are able to transform into human beings.

In this ambitious collection, the poems are interconnected. The ink from Cusac's pen goes incredibly deep into the archetypal realm. The lyrical evolves into story, and story evolves into voice, and the dramatic voices evolve into mythic resonance. This is big poetry. Not shimmery self-consciousness. Not superficial playfulness. Not ineffable shrines to the quotidian.

This poetry is as fundamental as rocks.

It captures a terrible longing and a powerful want. Its themes are terrifyingly powerful and disturbingly beautiful. Visceral excavations. Cataclysmic evocations. Our bodies blur as we stumble on the border between magic and fear:

> *But the ocean batting her ankles tells her*
> *it would fill every orifice,*
>
> *complete her forever,*
> *like that wet creature,*
>
> *that piece of the ocean,*
> *if only she would let it.*

This collection has the heft of a novel and the lightness of breath. It can shock by its primordial qualities and thrill by its art. As soon as you think you know what this poetry is, it becomes something else. This is a poetry of fusion where opposites join—where mystery and materiality merge. We all become

...the girl
who screwed a myth, screwed a song,
screwed a fish eater, screwed a beach pest.

Ultimately the human being is the hybrid creature. Animal and brain. Heart and hunger. Voice and vessel. Cusac's poetry grasps the huge themes: love and death and nature ("Nature used her/to make one more thing it has never made before.")

Hypnotic. Alluring. These poems are about becoming and becoming other. Ultimately this is a poetry of birth where we "stare/inside at the monster treading/water in her stomach."

By the end of this book, I doubt you'll agree that we need a new discipline to study it. But you will agree that Cusac's words will stay with you as you savor her story. Her book will transform into something else. It will evolve into a mythic creature, sensual and moving, uttering its own brilliant and strange story. Eventually, it will wear our skin.

Author's Preface

A Silkie is a mythical creature, a seal that leaves the ocean and takes human shape. Numerous ballads, many of them from Ireland and Scotland, tell stories about the supernatural beasts. The Silkies, who are more beautiful than mortals, surface to select and seduce lonely humans. They produce children, with the aim of returning with their progeny to the sea. They have one area of vulnerability; they need their coats in order to take the shape of seals and swim home.

The inhabitants of Atlantic Canada, many of whose ancestors came from Ireland and Scotland, still sing the ballads and, for centuries, had a sealing and fishing culture that sustained such music, along with the people. I first heard such a ballad, a version of "The Great Selkie o' Suleskerry," at a *ceilidh*, or party, performed by the College of Piping on Prince Edward Island. (The Maritime provinces include Prince Edward Island, New Brunswick, Nova Scotia, and Newfoundland.) Although many Silkie ballads concern female seals, the singer that night described a male Silkie who, after having sex with a young woman who falls asleep on a beach, and getting her pregnant in the process, offers to marry her. When she refuses him, he says he will give her a bag of gold after she has nursed their son for seven years. The woman in that ballad goes on with her life and marries a "gunner good," that is, a hunter. After the Silkie returns for her son, she learns from her husband that he has shot two seals—presumably for their meat and clothing. The gunner's victims are the Silkie and the woman's son. The ballad ends by registering her great grief.

The story I heard preoccupied me for months and eventually led to my attempt to tell a similar, though contemporized, tale.

Nova Scotia, Canada

I remember when I was a boy, any knocks at the door, I wouldn't let anybody go to the door but me. I knew there was nobody there that they could see. I knew the knocks were coming from that world. And I would always go to the door.

> —Cleve Townsend of Louisburg interviewed in *Down North: The Book of Cape Breton's Magazine,* edited by Ronald Caplan (Doubleday, 1980).

Contents

I. Wild Enough

wild enough	3
through the curtains	5
metamorphosis 1	7
gosling	9
silkie song	10
metamorphosis 2	11
spider	12
witness	13
dulsie sleeps	14
refrain	16

II. Economics Lesson

economics lesson	19
if she could change	22
the end of logic	23
theft	25
killdeer	27
evidence	28
leaving the gift	29
needle	30

III. Monster, Darling

tunnel	35
rumors	37
monster, darling	40
mother love	42
conceptus	43
suitor	45
gift	47
the list	49
silkie, naked	51

IV. Shooting the Dog

seal man	55
register	56
the beginning of revenge	57
shooting the dog	59
homecoming	63
as guns do	65

V. Epilogue

chasing the seal child	72
silkie song	75

Afterword   77

I

Wild Enough

wild enough

There were stories
    about girls wild enough,
        one in particular, Dulsie
            in her pale green halter, the faint
            shadows around her nipples, the way (we all noticed)
            they changed in the school air conditioning,

the school yard cigarette
    between her lips.
        Those lips
            could do anything: the scornful
            smile, the sneer, the break
            into warmth no one ever expected.

She could
    start screaming
        and still hold a cigarette
            in the corner of her mouth. When she
            breathed it in, her eyelids
            drooped, and she looked to the side, as if

she whom we thought
    so known, so physical,
        so summed
            in the calf muscles flexing, the wonderful
            body stretching from the arched
            foot through the fingers, all of her was lost

the moment
    she tasted
        the cigarette,
            and we didn't know her.
            Girls like her, wild enough
            to sleep alone on the beach,

not once for kicks,
    but again and again.
        The seals
            can spot a girl like that, can see
            the light her body throws off, and everything
            we miss about her body.

There were stories
    of how she woke
        in the dark
            and the sound of lapping waves. The tide
            crept almost to her feet but didn't
            touch her, and the body

six inches from hers
    wept its heat.
        It was the one
            she needed, the sand
            giving under her shoulders, right there.
            Later, she woke again, tide long out.

The body that
    had what?
        Loved her?
            was gone. In the shallows
            paddled a harbor seal,
            watching her the way they watch us.

through the curtains
(Mrs. Leighton)

Dulsie's hair is a bush
        the last sun
drums. I think, "She's
        caught fire," while under
tossing flames
        her forehead shines, and all of that
sex walks
        in front of my house.

One afternoon, she'll land
        in that same dress
on Barrington Street,
        Halifax, smiling hard
into the face of every
        man off the ferry.

Even our own boys
        hear the dress
talk. They wait
        in the slope between
salt marsh and dune
        squinting for
that hot,
        quivering hair.

We had a sheath knife in our belt, and a club—and when you'd see a seal you'd club him cross the nose and sell him. That's the way we done that. We'd pelt them right there.
—Jack Nicholson of St. Paul's Island interviewed in *Down North: The Book of Cape Breton's Magazine*, edited by Ronald Caplan (Doubleday, 1980).

metamorphosis 1

fissure fission

Don't imagine
the change in skin

slit snip scissor

from wet, thick, fatted

whittle hack

to papery and thin
doesn't cause pain.

spasm

Skull expands,
snout collapses,

twitch wrench hinge

limbs split off, spit out

pang slash tear crick

smooth trembling branches.

kink hitch cramp

Don't imagine
it doesn't excite him.

nip prick stitch

The sparse, crinkled
body hairs, the erection
full the moment he is born

thrill bite

into the miracle body
he finds useful only
for loving her
as he ducks his head,
careens beach-ward,

tweak split prune pare

shallows tripping him.

gosling

(Clyde MacLeod, Dulsie's father)

All that first night I think, "I should have stopped her."
Just before light, I hear her door latch catch
and the way she can't help clearing the outside air
from her throat, and her dropped keys on the chair.

Can a father control a daughter? She's smart in school
and yet she fools with her life, like a battery toy
she wants to break and put back together. Her dead mother
couldn't do better. So the next night I make my bed

outside her door. I dream of geese.
She vaults me as I wake. The wind from her foot
beats close like a wing, and I stare and see just motion
as if the darkness hurries down the staircase.

silkie song

(Silkie)

She flames like a window at evening
her hair the color of late sunset
so low and molten it drips into the water.

I shake myself hard
and follow the coldest current
until I see the mackerel
running for open water,

stomachs fat with the heat they've eaten,
gills streaming light like notched lanterns.

I pound my tail. I catch one
and another, another, another.
I tear into their bodies
until I cramp with belly fire
the color of her hair.

metamorphosis 2

(Scot Boyd)

She grips us,
her outlandish stamp
on the blacktop
pivots our brains,
and the way she nips
her words, bites
her lip, makes marks
in the tangerine
lipstick while informing
the teacher, "Cathay
means China,
not Carthage,"
then walks out
on the exam, but
now she gives
her own thoughts
the attention
she once gave us—it's not sex,
that's too easy,
but not *not* sex.

Her current
still travels across us
the way a rank vine
infects a wall. We want her back—
her old, bold cigarette
before the bell, blue
jeans ratted at the knees,
and, with those, her dependable,
almost mechanized
flickering gaze upon us. We'll
annihilate her otherwise.

spider

(Scot Boyd)

Out of half dark, loping with low hung head,
she crosses from the dune path down to the nine
tight little fires a crowd from school has lit.
We bunch, hunching our beers into our coats.
She leaps the first fire as if lifted on silk
and a slight in-breath, headlong to the fog—
lit, striped, short skirt, coiled calf, and ankle tendon—
drifts down, legs crooking, lands, keeps
running to the next fire, jumps it, doesn't
miss a one. Wind quickens the flames at her thighs.
She makes the last, falls hard, coughs in her sleeve
till the silk thread tugs her spine upright again.
We look at one another and don't speak.
She rubs her knee, leaves. We settle in our coats.
Old odors sigh from the fabric to our faces.

witness

One night, her Silkie asks her to watch him change.
And she knows she has won a precious license
to witness transformations she thinks wretched:
the seal fur that won't cover his nakedness,
though he fumbles as if he could button it up;
next, his collapse, chest and chin drive at the sand
right at the wave line, arms jerk, hands clenched and cupped
the way people die on TV. Still, the skin
contracts, rich-dark, his back hairs lift in the friction.
He's muscled, rounded, smooth, everything she wants.
The small waves rock him. He strains to reach the ocean,
then, with a lascivious flipper flash, he's gone.

She shivers when she thinks of the way he leaves her,
and feels too thin, as though made out of paper.

dulsie sleeps

Afternoons, the teacher in his lounge, we wait for her blazing
sleep. She compacts herself at her desk. We watch hundreds
of her slow breaths, see in them sexual
evidence. We know why she naps.

It is not just punishment, but recognition
of her singleness when Torie Loving takes scissors
one afternoon to Dulsie's hair, severs it, shags it
in eight slices, so the leftovers spike, twig,

the mass shudders and drops, and Torie lunges
for it, snatches it up, sniffs it,
binds it in brown rubber bands, plunges
it into her backpack, leaves the room.

Dulsie sleeps through the haircut with small, hard,
ignorant obstinacy. She wakes when the teacher comes back.
Her face gleams, sharpened, as her hand seeks
her hair, combs and, when the hair ends, keeps combing.

No one tells. We all, even Dulsie, even Torie Loving,
serve five nights of detention. Weeks later,
Torie brings in a needlepoint pillow
"Stuffed," her whisper, "with human remains."

She shows off her project above her head.
She's stitched a white, bright, whiskered, big-eyed face,
and, in turquoise and umber floss, all capitals, "HARP SEAL."
She smiles, picks hairs from the pillow, drops them.

The whole class turns toward Dulsie, but she is sleeping.

refrain

(Clyde MacCleod, Dulsie's father)

More seals
than weeds in the driveway, more
seals than fish,
more seals than jobs. They've won,
the seals.

II

Economics Lesson

economics lesson

Her words a single
        chewed chord,
                she informs him

people in this town
        hate hair seals, harp seals,
                gray, harbor, whatever

because they fatten,
        breed,
                and still hunger,

because the waves don't
        wash away
                enough of their excrement,

because fish
        slip whole
                down their gullets,

because the boats
        drag their nets all day,
                wash the blood

from their decks,
        not empty
                but with half the catch

they used to manage.
        People can't stop staring
                at their own paint-faded houses.

Again her hands
        grab her hair,
                measure

the length of grief.
        Nothing's fair,
                she says, but seals

infest the beach,
        laze, mate,
                bark on their bellies.

She throttles
        and flaps a hair lump.
                Shorn ends

prickle his nose,
        and the Silkie starts back
                with a terror.

"See what they did?"
        she asks, "See why
                they did it?"

I said to the boss one day, I'd like to try a flipper. He said, Well you can go up and ask the cook but I wouldn't. Me and the cook was pretty good friends. I went in and I said—her name was Mrs. MacMillan—Would you mind cooking a flipper for me? What are they like, she says? Smell? Aw, I don't think, I says. All right, she says, I'll try them, and God help you, she says, if they're smelly. After half an hour or so a fellow says to go on up now and see what she's like. Jeez, I went in she was lying on the lounge with an apron over her head. I says, How're you getting on? You fly the hell out of here, you and your darn flippers. But we had the flippers. I liked the flippers. They were good.

—Jack Nicholson of St. Paul's Island interviewed in Down North: The Book of Cape Breton's Magazine, edited by Ronald Caplan (Doubleday, 1980).

if she could change

But the night she really tries,
when he begins to shudder and shift
and she runs to him and pulls him
heavily onto her, willing whatever alchemy
makes him differ so from himself
to change her, too, his torso pounds
the breathing out of her lungs.
The new face tips and takes her in,
surprised, indifferent.

That's the instant she knows nothing
worthwhile has happened.

And she spits angry sobs because she is still herself.
The Silkie pushes from her.
The sun breaks along the back
of his swimming skull.

the end of logic

One early morning, coming home
tousled, damp-headed,
she meets her father at the door,

studies his evaluating eyes,
and understands she is a statistical error.

Dismissible, she has become
a new type of creature, an aberration;

the need creeping along her lips
is not anything
anyone calls "real."

*God made you. And God looked down
and hated what He had made
and, with a long hand, cast it to the side.*

Why suddenly the mirror? Why does
she have to look hard at herself,

scrutinize her filling thighs, the breasts
she isn't used to yet, the pubic curls,

the feet carrying her again and again
to the seal who mates with human girls?

*The legal code doesn't apply
to impossibilities.*

Or not carrying her there
because now she won't, she won't
go to the strip of salt and silt

where he waits for the tide, not for her.

*But the law
simply doesn't apply*

So she gives in. She follows the road,
though no road leads to a creature that can't exist.

*God's long hand, His loose fingers
graze the sand.*

She calms herself by thinking, "Nobody
does things that don't happen."

But the ocean batting her ankles tells her
it would fill every orifice,

complete her forever,
like that wet creature,

that piece of the ocean,
if only she would let it.

theft

Late at night, she separates her body,
        leaves him dozing, hitches up
her cutoffs, yanks down the T-shirt,
        forgets her shoes, runs for home.
The piled sealskin trips her, and she gasps,
        fur spiking her calf
wet, oiled, sand-crusted. His smell,
        but stronger, submerges her, waves of it lapping,
and her insides lurch with desire
        for what, in the darkness, she can't make out lying there
until, thinking *of him of him*, she gathers
        the folds of skin to her chest. The smell appalls her,
its raw, watery meatiness. Her cheek flinches
        at the clammy underside. But by now she has found
she can't put it down.
        It weighs as much as two six-packs.
In the streetlight, fur pricks
        and glitters. Voracious, she drinks
the smell, beastly, nearly human.
        This, she thinks, *is what we want.*

He showed us how to sculp them and leave the fat right on the hide. We'd clip them in the tow. We'd lace a rope through the eyes. Well, if they were heavy or big, four would be a load to haul on the ice, you know. It was slippery, of course, the fur was slippery, and that's the way we used to get them into the land.

>—Jack Nicholson of St. Paul's Island interviewed in *Down North: The Book of Cape Breton's Magazine,* edited by Ronald Caplan (Doubleday, 1980).

killdeer

The moon was skinny to begin with. Now
clouds muffle it so he can't see his own hand.
That's why, when he reaches the little hollow

where, he swears, he left his sealskin,
and it is not there, he trusts
his attenuated brain,

as if his nerve fibers begin
along the spine and end in the skin
so, wherever it is, it draws him.

Only now, for the first time,
he can't feel it
in the opening behind his mind.

He picks up speed,
sniffs the breeze
from hollow to hollow.

All the while his hands work sand,
and the slow absence starts
in the space below his heart.

By daybreak, he runs naked
between the dunes
like a cursed sand bird.

evidence

When he asks if she has seen his seal coat, she laughs
first in her throat, then deeper as she raises
palm to his chest hairs, rubs them, tangles
her fingertips, releases, bends
nose to his midriff, inhales.

Her skin tickles him mildly, but that's not what
makes him join her in hissed giggles
that dive into his belly until
he cackles, yells
release, and can't breathe

in enough before the next convulsion
makes him desperate.
No, it's not the tickle.
It's recognizing in her throat sound
both an admission of guilt and enough of a lie for safety.

leaving the gift

She glances about for her Silkie while she folds
and piles the simple wardrobe she planned
lovingly—pleated trousers, long gray coat,
shined shoes—on the still-hot, cooling sand.

It's an exchange: clothes that will make him human,
clothes that will change his nature and his smell,
all that for the long, heavy fur skin
that means he cannot leave her, and she's won.

As she bends to adjust a sleeve, she breathes the scent
of her father's closet, which reeks of his hair oil.
The rich smell almost displeases her. And yet,
as she tucks money in the coat sleeve, straightens, toils

up the sand toward town, what she has done
thrills her and twists and flutters in her intestines.
So when she turns and spots her love at the wave-line,
she hesitates before she continues home.

needle

She must
        not realize
                as she paws
      him, must
have no idea
      anguish
              already stitches
      his insides. If
he had his seal skin,
      she couldn't
             make him feel
     or flinch
before the needle,
      anticipate
             when she arcs above him
      and he rages
in love and malignant
      sorrow under
             the broom fringe
                  of her—in the dropping
            darkness—
    garnet
hair.

III

Monster, Darling

tunnel

(Mrs. Willie Babinot)

I'm seventy-two. That's old enough
to remember, not too old to tell you
he's here again, walking too slowly
to be useful. Not someone like him. The exact
man, same caves along his collarbone.
Noticing, I felt my mouth
right then, hunger for oranges.

Long ago, I met him while eating
the fourth orange of my life
on the Marguerite picnic ground.
All my walk there, paper
wrappers brushed my ankles, lifted
sharp smells, memory
of sugar.

I'd go hungry two days for such a fruit,
yet I bought it, weighed it,
bored my hole, squeezed drops
to my tongue, sucked, sat,
didn't see the booths, pants legs dusty,
pups nipping each other, until
my mouth hurt, the orange stopped giving,

and I looked up. He stood there, so pretty,
head tipped just like a seal in a bay—
same head that passed me yesterday,
that couldn't bring itself to recognize
my face buried behind this face,
my body lost in the folds of a body
that ran to him once, that carried bébé

until she died and I wished I would, and Maman
wouldn't let me see my own
newborn "female monster,"
said if I saw her I'd never sleep again,
and planted bébé with pinks and didn't tell me.
Years later, I dug there and found
the whole, perfect human skeleton.

Once old Yvette saw me on his arm
and yelled from her porch, "Venez!"
I went to her and she, in bulging black
and cerise wool, said, "He was mine,"
nodded at him, "Weren't you?"
We left. She called out twice, "Chéri!"
I didn't believe her then, but later,

after bébé died, I strengthened
enough to be vain and check my hairdo,
peering into two mirrors. That's when
I saw the tunnel their reflections made
and I gazed into the future, into
the past, and saw in both directions, repeated,
the front and the back of a woman's head.

rumors

Scot caught up and, though she kept
walking, took Dulsie's waist

in his hands, under the parka, right on the dress.
The heat of her stopped

the cramps in his fingers. Dulsie bent
over and spat on his shoe.

He had thought she wanted anyone.
He watched her

for three years, waiting
for the seconds she looked up

full into the eyes of whoever
would meet hers

then lowered her chin, smiling
back at the page.

But the gob sliding
slow as her smile,

slow as his wish, plopped
right on his shoe-top.

At the beach bottom
he turned back and saw her

scramble for a man, and they wrestled
together into the small waves.

      A man? Torie says
      it's a seal,

          out of the water just for Dulsie. How would you
          like your own seal?

Scot saw a man. He wanted to bash his skull.
He thought of the collapsed head

there in the wash.
But he went home instead.

          When they shake themselves like dogs,
          her hair sprays sand,

          but clots stick to her curls, with seaweed
          tucked in like hairpins.

We should catch the thing,
wrap it

up for her pretty and see
what Dulsie does.

That night—it was a moonlight fine night. The first ice was struck, she started to go like this. Rocking. And we were at seals that night. . . . And next morning we got ninety.
      —Theodore Rideout interviewed in *Cape Breton Lives: A Book from Cape Breton's Magazine,* edited by Ronald Caplan (Breakwater Books, 1988).

monster, darling

1.
The day Dulsie first suspects
there must be something

else inside her, the word
keeps entering her ear

in an intimate, chummy voice
she thinks of as a new friend. "Impossible,"

and she understands
that what could inhabit

her is impossible when she straightens
her blouse, ambles to the chalkboard,

gets the trig problem right and the voice
trills happily in her ear.

"Impossible," her transparent
clothing and skin,

or that her classmates could stare
inside at the monster treading

water in her stomach.

2.
"Impossible" at night as wind whips sand
so grains lodge

in the whorls of her ear.
Her Silkie finds and nips

her jawbone, so her body
responds, and she imagines

stopping herself, sand
burying her ear like a dead shell

while the loud ocean
will soon get to her ear

so it won't hear the word, or
anything but percussion.

3.
The monster sculls with its miniature fins,
cute, like a cartoon horror, a pet

she didn't ask for but adores anyhow.
In her fishbowl stomach

the small brown swimmer she scarcely
spots in the dark, tethered

on its umbilical hose, circles,
scratches the walls,

hunts
for an opening.

mother love

Somehow the infant house-finch, despite the lolling head,
the bulging black-coated eyes, the beak
that weighs too much and keeps dragging the skull forward
while another force (could it be, this young, the will?)
pulls the whole head momentarily upright, blind eyes seeking light,
somehow it doesn't
spill itself out of the nest.

It's ugly: the pink-and-yellow beak sprouting hairs
and the mostly naked head like a shrunken ostrich, but
people say this every spring, its mother loves it, finds it
dearer than any face she has seen until this instant
of recognition, *ah, you, there you are.*
Still, Dulsie thinks to herself,
is this love or must love—

caged love, need love, love that
nature invents to feed itself as it grows
more lush, distended
with humidity, feathered, furred so that even
she and the life swimming inside her
are one more trick
of fecundity?

Was that what happened? Nature used her
to make one more thing it has never made before?
She doesn't even show yet, but
people say every spring, *its*
mother loves it, as the pink-and-yellow
beak opens
and begs for food.

conceptus

(Clyde Macleod, Dulsie's father)

Someone said to me, a man
at my job . . . my desk job. No,
the boat I put out
all on its own. It broke up
over Lunenburg. Thought I'd
refill the ocean.
He actually
said, "your daughter
humps seals, and the reason
for all of the sweatshirts is—
have a look at her tummy."
So I asked her, "What the hell
have you got going on
inside there—an aquarium?"
She blew her breath at my eyes,
backed up, left. Of course,
she went to the beach.
She told that damn seal
our little joke as if it meant
that I hadn't
reared her well, fed her,
talked her back to sleep
after those dreams
about the angry tree.
All that, you build it
together into love.
I know her favorite
kiddo socks, red train engines.
She'd catch them up in two hands.
I had to pry away her fingers
to put them on her feet.
The thing that gets me—now
he whistles for her and she

goes, now she's set
on changing into someone else—
no one remembers her
the way I do.
I remember a child you've never seen
hauling lines, sniffing waves.
The delight got even
into her hair. And stubbornness,
right to the hair ends.
Do you want to know
what else the guy at my office said?
"One more seal baby.
It makes me wonder
how much of the town
is sealish." And, you know,
I believe him,
though I tell myself there are reasons
we don't trust those old stories
or even tell them anymore,
but when I notice
the way she favors
her stomach (is she really,
could she be,
protecting it?),
his voice starts
knocking back of my head,
and I know everything
he said is true.

suitor

The Silkie sifts coins in his coat pockets
as he comes to a stop at her stoop, fingers grabbing
the money in a bunch, letting it drop.

She's set herself into the corner of the couch, hidden
despite her oversize belly, though the words
still find her out, as if the muscle of her ear has cramped
on the syllables her father
shouted from across the yard, days ago now,
"You bring that thing home alive, I'll kill it," as she studied
without seeming to do so, the block's dark windows
that wouldn't tell her who
among the neighbors heard, who didn't.

The Silkie waits. She hears the silver talking
with the cool wind over the sill
and thirsts, looks up through the window
while confusion scours her mind.

Yet she lets the door slam, stands with her feet apart
in front of the thin man in her father's clothes,
in front of the dark windows in late afternoon,
and thinks, *with a belly this size,*
I can't hide, not here, and readies herself
to tell him, "Even though
they talk about me behind their windows,
I can't marry you."
                        But he doesn't ask.

He waits until she wonders what he's doing there,
gray-lipped, with a new-shaved face on the stoop.
Then he tells her, "You'll have our daughter for seven years.
I'll come back for her

and pay you for your trouble." He turns away
while dread closes like a womb over her womb,
and she says, "What?
What did you say there, what?"

As he walks, the silver talking
starts again with a chafe and jangle
and she watches the brown head and loose clothing
striding without her
as her ear longs for the sound,
as she drives him from her mind.

gift

It's not until
Dulsie shrugs on her coat
shuts the door hard
turns her back on the house
lets her enlarged
stomach lead
down the driveway
as her darkening
nipples chafe in her shirt,
and at the road
swerves right,
hoping to run into no one,
that the brown lump
in the crosswalk
makes her frown.

It might be a body in a coat,
a child in a blanket,
and she strides toward it.

When she's almost
upon it, the shape resolves
into a seal bound
in fishnet choked
round and round the torso
as if someone took care
to truss it, tuck in the ends.
She stops, she looks
about her. No one.

It's a nursing female,
teats engorged,
one pinched, twisted

in netting, so Dulsie
falls on her knees
as the smell of death
enfolds her, and she,
with both hands, fingers
pressing the cold nipple,
frees the teat,
only the teat.

the list

(Torie Loving)

Did you see? She talks to her stomach
like a great dog she's scared of, making promises
alone in the market aisles, not caring who hears
the grocery list she's cursed to read forever,
singing, "Gold-eyed bird, backhoe, new oats, you won't
ever go hungry, peach sugar, barley." Scot
gets up behind her, spies, comes back with, "It's dishes today,"
or "cod cakes, quahog, little neck, mackerel running."

Scot doesn't love her now, but one day he told Dulsie
what she was, and his voice cracked on "whore."
He doubled over, roared at the ground, hair hanging—
a big guy, six feet maybe, grabbing his own knees.
She petted his back. He said "Don't touch me,"
but stayed there, and she drew her hand
along his spine until he forced himself to stand
and left her to talk alone to her baby.

Came a storm from the southeast, thick-a-snow. And old Capt. Marley from Trinity Bay, Newfoundland, was the captain of the ship. He blew the whistle and all hands went on board. He started up the Gulf. Went for 4 days and 4 nights—the vessel—through the ice. We went up, I guess up around Anticosti, the other side of—you couldn't see any land, anyway. And we got stuck. And there we lay in one spot for 6 weeks and 3 days.
   —Theodore Rideout interviewed in *Cape Breton Lives: A Book from Cape Breton's Magazine,* edited by Ronald Caplan (Breakwater Books, 1988).

silkie, naked

He meets up with the skinned seal at daybreak
in the skinny man framed in the skinny mirror
on the skinny rented door. He has new fingers
that work much harder than they should to bunch
and draw the borrowed pants up his thighs,
to breathe slowly, to snap, to buckle, to learn
how to button so the collar hems match,
as his anxiety rises, as the dry
edges of his eyes pinch and then relax.

But he continues, like one of Death's possessions
that fell through a hole in a pocket. The years slide by,
the worn pants leg begins to feel like his,
and Death's hand, still fumbling in its pocket,
the hand he almost loves, can't find him now.

III

Shooting the Dog

seal man

"Seal man!" yells the child in the restaurant high chair
that he, in his white apron, passes with his burden
of hot white plates, his eyes seizing the child's
as Dulsie jolts from her seat to block his view.
"Seal man!" glee in the shrill trill, the small
fingers grab for his hair after Dulsie scoops
the struggling toddler up against her shoulder,

and her elbow flings out a diaper bag, which knocks him,
and he staggers under his busboy's tray
so the teaspoon he drops makes a little jingle
that runnels across his mind with the sensation
of Dulsie in a blouse of worn, sheer cotton,
of Dulsie, whose body turns the other direction.

register

She tells herself she is taking the job
because they'll have to speak
to her politely, as if she isn't their fear
in a stiff, red apron punching the register.

Their fear. The girl they think of
more than they should, the girl
who screwed a myth, screwed a song,
screwed a fish eater, screwed a beach pest.

A girl who will stand for the rest of the day
in her heels and red apron, who once
thought too much of herself, who made a mistake
she pushes in a stroller through the town.

Before that, Silkie was a tune they hummed in the kitchen
to keep their minds off the dishes,
a memory the kids sang in the auditorium,
the special soloist wrenching the words,

though still
the sound touched them
for some reason,
the old piano notes, the old idea

of a creature who comes from the ocean
to comfort the town women, to manufacture
more and more charmed children.
Myth. Song. Fish eater. Pest.

the beginning of revenge

He lifts his feet so slowly, cough
digging at his lungs, that Dulsie,
whenever she hears the sound, heads off
down the sidewalk without looking.
Yet, on a day of wet grass, when he comes upon
his daughter Briane in soaked tennies in her yard,
no Dulsie rushes from the house when his cough
startles the child, and she stares up at him.

And when he asks her if she has seen a fur
like a seal without a seal inside it,
"In the basement! Hanging in the basement!"
is her shout, and no Dulsie snatches
Briane from springing up the stoop. A neighbor
mows a square yard without looking up.
The child returns, lugging the skin behind her,
and dumps it at his feet. "Do I get a quarter?"

But he can't stop the terror in his answer,
"I'll return. Don't tell. I'll be
back in a week to pay you,"
his lungs pumping, his feet pounding
away from the girl in purple overalls
and the red straggles of hair, while his weeping
against his lost skin and his lost smell,
coats his tongue with the taste of his own musk.

You had to go way out on the ice. You'd have to go out and get among the seals—they were thick, thousands of them.
>—Jack Nicholson of St. Paul's Island interviewed in *Down North: The Book of Cape Breton's Magazine,* edited by Ronald Caplan, (Doubleday, 1980)

shooting the dog

Shooting a seal, Dulsie thinks, is like
shooting a dog:

the inexplicable
forgiveness

of the dog, obsessively licking his side,
who crawls into the lap

of his murderer to roll his eyes
in dependence and pain

and adoration, to shudder,
to pause a long time

between breaths.

So, on her good days, when she
tells herself that to win

she must imagine winning,
she takes the lady's

pistol from its case, cradles
the pearl gray muzzle

against her cheek, and is almost
elated at its cool power

to put everything
right.

In the version of the story
she tells herself,

on the day he comes to steal her daughter,
she startles, lets go of the page,

so the book leaps like a white wing,
and her face brightens in the doorway daylight

as she detects the future on the stoop.
Her shot is true,

and, though he enters the house
backlit, upright, an ordinary beautiful man,

when he collapses, he is brown soft fur
creeping to her feet

where he half loops like a lazy capital *C*
in her little girl's script. She goes tipsy

with compassion, sits cross-legged
to examine the hole she made,

and the seal inhales, launches his body
into her lap, sighs, rolls his eyes.

In the story she tells herself,
she strokes his head until he dies.

When the carcass has cooled,
she uses Briane's Radio Flyer

to haul the velvet sack to the beach.
No one sees her, and she stands there

regretting
his necessary death

as the brown waves comb his side
and the caked blood loosens and leaks.

Because she does these things
between the hours of three and six a.m.

her daughter doesn't wake up
until after she returns and scrubs the floor.

§ § §

But every story has phantom lives
that must breathe and act out,

and other versions flicker
at the fringe of her sight.

There is the dog who understands
his master is his murderer,

who barks at the hand that pets him
and slinks under the car to die.

There is the seal who never
returns to claim his daughter.

There is the woman
who wastes her life waiting.

There is the bloated, dead
beautiful man.

There is the little girl who wakes.

homecoming

Before the end of the story, there is joy
in the hand that trusts his, fits in his palm hotly,
stickily, damply, tinily, loosely. Briane can't
keep hold at the more jarring steps,
and gloms onto her father's jacket hem. The instant
his daughter catches the fabric, the Silkie sees
Dulsie's hand, the fingers, even
in miniature, too long for their palms
as they rub, crunch, and pleat the jacket canvas.
His daughter's hands, his own hand, Dulsie's—
all of these together as precious
as storms of alewives, as sun baking
droplets from his skin, as open sea
when he plunges under, and the depths sprawl
beneath him like rooms of mirrors.

Dulsie is at their backs. Joy, desire, joy
fold on him as one wave engulfs another
each time he dares to turn and glimpse her
in her red, slim jacket, orange locks tangling
along her breasts. He sees, he adores,
though she no longer wants him,
though she follows at a distance
not hollering, not begging for their daughter.

The last of the asphalt founders under sand.
Briane's voice rushes. Big strides. She lets the coat-hem go.
The Silkie's neck hair pricks. He loves this too much.
He thinks it means the three of them are cursed,
though the sealskins lie in the hollow where he left them.
The girl shrieks, "Costume!" wriggles
so the fur humps and draggles at her ankles.
Then Briane freezes and cries out.

Pain melts her legs together. She falls
onto one hip, rolls, catches
herself with an elbow, which collapses
to a stump, its black claws flapping.
The Silkie shudders at the scene.
He hadn't imagined a face rucked in pain,
a little body thudding, when he thought
of family throngs nuzzling the pup in welcome.
The girl mews, but her father's still-human ears
can't understand; he shivers, clasps
his own skin, and the dark barking
rises in his throat. His jawbones lengthen.
He feels again the stab
of losing a body to gain one
as he blinks and remembers a woman
even as human feeling slips from him.

Hours or seconds? Dulsie at his skull,
her lips purse and clench, her language
hammers his ear skin, she's too close,
too close, and he can't understand her,
though he pauses, thrilling at the sound.
Only his nostrils flare at her stench.
Her mouth approaches his eye.
The lip skin puckers; he sees tongue buds.
He has to go.
Daughter and father hunch and haul their tails
while Dulsie flings words at their heads,
but they are almost home, glass smashing
to liquid over them. The Silkie tastes salt.
The pup yelps, yelps in pleasure.

as guns do

The one
in her hand
goes off

four times.
Every muscle
in her clenches.

The bullets
she can't follow
dive, swim, drown.

The sound.
The echo. She hears
too many

and whirls, sees
her father above
her on a dune,

sees Scot from school
nod at her father
fiercely,

hears Torie Loving
somewhere
laugh.

Oh.
She returns.
Days. Weeks.

She never
finds
sign

of her bonny, her
wee
babe.

V

Epilogue

Well, it's starvation. We had starvation on the ship. And all kinds of meat aboard of her. Twenty-five quarters of meat going spoiling—big western quarters of meat—we didn't get any. Only the captain was getting that, and officers and doctors. . . . If we'd have got some seals, I guess we'd have got some good grub.

  —Theodore Rideout interviewed in *Cape Breton Lives: A Book from Cape Breton's Magazine*, edited by Ronald Caplan (Breakwater Books, 1988).

chasing the seal child

1.
Her love harsh as twine,
she rows, grimaces,
stares. Somewhere ahead, she's sure,
though her memories weigh so much they'd
double her body if she let them,
the slippery child
spanks the surface with her tailfin,
lunging, bopping higgledy-piggledy—

the daughter once kept from the sea—
a confiding secret four blocks away,
so Briane would ask at night, as Dulsie
reached to switch off the lamp,
"What is that sound like breathing?"
Spatter of freckles, sweet sweat smell,
tucked hair, fake tortoiseshell barrette,
the strong, small, unstopping body
stomping through rooms of daylight,
the child who slept so hard at night,
who now can't drown.

On any other day, Dulsie would resent the wind
forcing her eyes closed, despise
that smack on her face. Today,
the cold smart of it tells her she
has her own heat; and the wind hurts her
because she once felt pleasure.

If her skin aims across the water
its spiky, varying light,
her Silkie will notice her body glimmer, need her
again, power to the surface,

crash to her on the surf,
nuzzle her with his sopping, gamy fur.
How she will seize him this time,
clench his slithery dripping against her
as she wrenches and wrings
him with desire. She'll kill that immortal thief
for hours, until he knows
what mortality feels like,
until the curious-eyed child
in the wrong body
sweeps to them, barking instead of giggling.
Then she'll let go.

2.
Wind stiffens her nipples, flutters of water
bouncing the boat to Seal Island,
where, she's sure,
Briane yips, skids down
the slope of a flat stone
and flips into waves.

The longing grief in Dulsie's throat
pushes the dinghy
out beyond the reef.
She heaves the oars. The effort
creases her belly, trembles her breasts.
Hair sticks darkened tendrils along her jaw.

The losses of her life dive through her.
She watches them plummet,
strange, furtive creatures.
The island wind delivers its stench of seals.
The adults loll, bristle, honk.

Dulsie aches, waits for an aching cry
back at her. But all the pups are the same
downy brown, slinking, polished.
She yells "Briane," and all the pups gaze up.
She throws a leg over the gunwale,
hisses, pulls it out again.
The water is winter.

If she dives, her blood will stiffen,
rocks will chew the keel,
the seals will slice the waves,
throng upon her,
sniff her thickening body, reject it.
It's futile. She hates them.

She yanks the oars,
sees the shore town in red moonlight
the far-off empty red-lit beach,
her life without a seal skin in her basement,
without the feral human
starving because she loved him,
without the orange-haired daughter
running back to her.

They are wild.
They can't think of her,
though once, in a small boat of arched white pine
his heat tumbled against her
like that of a human lover,
though once she hollered her birth pain
like any other human mother.

silkie song

(Silkie)

At sundown, shoes and stockings in her hand,
as ocean fingertips scratch the sand,
the woman with nut-brown hair stands laughing
while the tide clasps her ankles as I would clasp her ankles.

I swallow the motion
when wind flicks the nylon along her calf.
She almost lets the shoes drop
then catches them to her chest as if day could begin over

while the sun pauses, half sunken,
and she would sit on the sand to work the stocking
saturated with the soil of one day
over the arch of her foot to start another.

Afterword

My mother is from the Maritimes. My parents and large extended family live there today. I have heard a great deal about seals over the years, much of the talk sorrowful and angry.

During the 1970s, the environmental organization Greenpeace targeted the hunting of harp seals in Newfoundland. Particularly in the United States, the group distributed images of the appealing, dark-eyed, white-coated pups, which, Greenpeace emphasized, hunters were bludgeoning to death. The stories were true, and inadequate, conveying neither the cultural depth of the hunt nor the precarious economic life of the Newfoundlanders.

The seal fur market collapsed in response to the campaign. Two-week old pups, those with the white coats popular in the fur trade, became protected animals. The Newfoundlanders, many already impoverished, lost a centuries-old way of life and a source of income.

The Maritimers have complaints about the Greenpeace campaign, among them accusations that Greenpeace exploited the adorable faces of the pups and did not consider the well-being of the Newfoundlanders.

Newfoundlanders continued to hunt the older seals according to an annual quota. But the harp seal population exploded. By the early 1990s, the Atlantic Canada cod stocks had dropped significantly. Perhaps a poster I purchased on Cape Breton Island, Nova Scotia, captures best what the loss of this source of food and income meant to Maritimers: Below a photograph of a cod the size of a human, it said, "In Cod We Trusted." Many Maritimers, still resentful about the end of the seal hunt, blame the seals for the loss of the fish, and the loss of their ability to make a living by fishing. "The seals eat all the fish," is a common complaint with truth to it. (The whole truth is, of course, more complicated, involving human activities, especially those of large fishing ships on international waters, as well as seal hunger.) For many Maritimers, seals have plunged in status from a source of food and clothing, a partner in the hard northern life, to an animal akin to a rodent, crowding and polluting beaches, and eating too much.

The controversy, now decades old, has not gone away. In April 2004, Greenpeace published on its web site this announcement:

> Newfoundland, Canada—The Canadian government has approved a massive expansion in the allowable catch for harp seals in Canada to a maximum of 350,000 animals this year. While 'whitecoat' harp seals (under 2 weeks old) are still protected as a result of actions by Greenpeace and other organisations in the 70s and 80s, and some of the more extreme animal rights abuses have been outlawed, older seals can still be legally hunted under Canadian law.
>
> This year's quota is the highest for any year since 1967. Canada's cod fishery collapsed in the early 90s, and some in Canada blamed the seals, despite the fact that the greatest culprit was clearly decades of human overfishing. The collapse of fisheries around Newfoundland due to mismanagement are a major driver in the economics of expanding the seal hunt—and part of an all too predictable cycle of "exploit, deplete, and move on" which have characterised human commercial hunts of wild animals the world over.

In that same month, Greenpeace announced that it would target more pressing concerns, including global warming and genetically modified organisms, and would no longer campaign against the Newfoundland seal hunt. The Humane Society of the United States has, however, continued to mount a yearly protest on the Gulf of St. Lawrence ice floes. In 2006, Paul McCartney and his then-wife, Heather Mills McCartney, traveled to the floes to pose with days-old whitecoat seals. Paul McCartney described the hunt as a "stain on the character of the Canadian people." Images of the McCartneys next to a baby seal were widely distributed, appearing in *USA Today* and on CBS news, among other media. The implication of the photos, that the baby seals were doomed to slaughter, prompted accusations of distortion from Newfoundlanders. Alan Doyle, a Newfoundland folk musician and member of the group Great Big Sea, accused the ice floe photo of being "misleading" and "unfair" to those careful "sealers in small struggling communities everywhere." In contrast to the implications of the photo, "there has not been a cute and cuddly baby seal hunt in a long long time," Doyle wrote on his group's web site. "Older harp seals are what the sealers are after but I'll bet these much uglier dudes won't make the final photo." Doyle ended with a grim goodbye to the former Beatle and his wife. "Well, Mr. and Ms. McCartney, enjoy your trip to Atlantic Canada. If your efforts today are really successful, there may be a few less towns to see next time you stop by."

Whatever one might think about the obligations of environmentalists to the human cultures they critique, the Maritime seal hunt is not an easy one to tuck away. The conflict between the environmentalists and, on the losing end, the cultural and economic life of Newfoundland has interested and saddened me for decades. It has not made me optimistic about the environmental movement, whose aims I, on the whole, support.

And so, on a May evening when I heard a ballad about love between a seal-man and a woman, I wondered what would happen if a young Maritimer, the daughter of a fisherman who has lost his work, ran into a Silkie today and decided to follow (in a contemporary society still grieving the loss of the old ways) the storyline of a myth derived from a hunting culture. The story of Dulsie and her Silkie is one of cultural betrayal for the sake of passion, sexual pleasure, wildness, and willfulness. It is also a story of love—albeit a hurting, twisting love—that pushes forward in spite of the opposition of an entire town.

Notes

Page 3:

Dulsie's name derives from dulse—a red, edible seaweed.

Page 5:

Barrington Street in Halifax runs parallel to the wharf and is known for prostitution.

Page 14:

Torie's needlepoint pillow refers to the Greenpeace seal campaign.

Page 19:

Harbor seals, grey seals, and harp seals are all earless seals—that is, they have no ear lobes. They swim by wriggling side to side, their tails functioning as rudders. These earless seals are also called hair seals. All hair seals are often thought of as pests and as destructive to commercial fishing stocks in the Canadian Maritimes.

Harbor seals tend to be common in harbors and along coastlines. They often watch humans but are cautious about coming ashore in populated areas. They have faces that resemble dogs, with eager, seeking eyes. As harbor seals often live near human towns, the Silkie myths most likely concern these seals.

Grey seals are larger than harbor seals. While the coats of harbor seals range from white and speckled to dark brown, grey seals are always spotted—females light with dark mottling, males dark with light mottling. Anyone who has traveled in Maritime waters probably has memories of grey seals in the motorboat wake, seeking churned-up fish and staring at the passengers.

Harp seals pass their summers in the Arctic and travel to the Gulf of St. Lawrence to give birth in wintertime. The young have white coats with a harp-like marking on the face. Later, the fur turns gray with dark mottling.

Page 26:

"Sculp" is a variant of "sculpt," and means "to carve." The sealers carve the seal out of its skin.

Page 27:

A killdeer is a type of plover, a coastal bird often found near human habitats. The killdeer drags its wing when threatened—a trick that lures predators away from the bird's nest.

Page 39:

"She" refers to a sealing ship. "At seals" means that the ship has reached the hunting grounds, so that the hunters can begin their kill the next morning.

About the author

Anne-Marie Cusac's poetry has appeared in *Poetry*, *Iowa Review*, *TriQuarterly*, *The American Scholar*, *The Madison Review*, and *Crab Orchard Review*. Her first poetry book, *The Mean Days* (2001) was published by Tia Chucha Press and won the Posner Book Award from the Council for Wisconsin Writers. A recipient of a Wallace Stegner Fellowship at Stanford University and a Wisconsin Arts Board Individual Artist's grant, Cusac was for ten years an editor and investigative reporter for *The Progressive* magazine. Her investigative reporting there won several awards, including the prestigious George Polk Award. As of fall 2006, she is a professor in Communication at Roosevelt University and a contributing writer for *The Progressive*.